FLANNEL AUTUMN ROADS COOKBOOK

Cranberry, Pumpkin and Apple Recipes

First Edition

By Tim Murphy

Copyright 2017
Shamrock Arrow Media

For information on Flannel John's Cookbooks and upcoming releases visit www.flanneljohn.com

FLANNEL JOHN'S AUTUMN ROADS COOKBOOK

Cranberry, Pumpkin and Apple Recipes

TABLE OF CONTENTS

CRANBERRY RECIPES_____**Page 9**
After Thanksgiving Turkey Sandwich____ Page 11
Apple Cider Cranberry Punch_____Page 12
Apple Cranberry Fluff_____Page 13
Apple Cranberry Pork Chops_____Page 14
Banana Cranberry Bread_____Page 15
Beef Tenderloin_____Page 16
Bog Punch_____Page 17
Cheese & Cranberry Cookies_____Page 18
Chicken Breast with Cranberries_____Page 19
Cocktail Sausages_____Page 20
Cranberry Almond Bread_____Page 21
Cranberry Applesauce_____Page 22
Cranberry Bars_____Page 23
Cranberry Bread_____Page 24

Cranberry Bread II	Page 25
Cranberry Cake	Page 26
Cranberry Carrots	Page 27
Cranberry Chutney	Page 28
Cranberry Chicken	Page 29
Cranberry Citrus Holiday Punch	Page 30
Cranberry Conserve	Page 31
Cranberry Cooler	Page 32
Cranberry Crisp	Page 33
Cranberry Currant Walnut Sauce	Page 34
Cranberry Frost	Page 35
Cranberry Ham Glaze	Page 36
Cranberry Honey Relish	Page 37
Cranberry Orange Pancake Syrup	Page 38
Cranberry Pecan Muffins	Page 39
Cranberry Pie	Page 40
Cranberry Pudding	Page 41
Cranberry Relish	Page 42
Cranberry Roast	Page 43
Cranberry Salad	Page 44
Cranberry Tea	Page 45
Cranberry Walnut Sauce	Page 46
Fresh Cranberry Salad	Page 47
Gorp	Page 48
Grandma's Cranberry Sauce	Page 49
Grilled Cheese Cranberry Sandwich	Page 50
Honey Pear Cranberry Sauce	Page 51
Hot Cranberry Autumn Punch	Page 52

Ilwaco Cranberry Salad_____Page 53
Orange & Ginger Cranberries_____Page 54
Peninsula Trail Mix_____Page 55
Pork Chops_____Page 56
Pork Tenderloin_____Page 57
Simple Cranberry Sauce_____Page 58
Slow Cooked Turkey Breast_____Page 59
Spiced Cranberry Tea_____Page 60
Spicy Cranberry Chutney_____Page 61
Tangy Cranberry Sauce_____Page 62
Turkey Breast_____Page 63
White Chocolate Cranberry Cookies_____Page 64

PUMPKIN RECIPES_____**Page 65**
Autumn Soup_____Page 67
Baked Pumpkin_____Page 68
Bean & Pumpkin Soup_____Page 69
Chicken Pumpkin Chili_____Page 70
Chocolate Chip Pumpkin Cake_____Page 71
Creamy Pumpkin Soup_____Page 72
Ginger Pumpkin Soup_____Page 73
Harvest Pumpkin Cake_____Page 74
Harvest Pumpkin Pie_____Page 75
Hidatsa Pumpkin_____Page 76
Honey Pumpkin Butter_____Page 77
Hot Pumpkin Eggnog_____Page 78
Jack O'Lantern Soup_____Page 79
Maple Pumpkin Cheesecake_____Page 80

No Bake Pumpkin Pie	Page 81
Orange Ginger Pumpkin Seeds	Page 82
Patch & Orchard Cocktail	Page 83
Pumpkin Bread	Page 84
Pumpkin Burgers	Page 85
Pumpkin Candy	Page 86
Pumpkin Casserole	Page 87
Pumpkin Chai Tea Latte	Page 88
Pumpkin Cornbread	Page 89
Pumpkin Fudge	Page 90
Pumpkin Granola	Page 91
Pumpkin Hickory Cake	Page 92
Pumpkin Hummus	Page 93
Pumpkin Meatloaf	Page 94
Pumpkin Muffins	Page 95
Pumpkin Mushroom Soup	Page 96
Pumpkin Oatmeal	Page 97
Pumpkin Pancakes	Page 98
Pumpkin Pickles	Page 99
Pumpkin Pie	Page 100
Pumpkin Pie Jell-O Shots	Page 101
Pumpkin Pie Milkshake	Page 102
Pumpkin Pie Fruit Leather	Page 103
Pumpkin Pie Popsicles	Page 104
Pumpkin Pine Nut Bread	Page 105
Pumpkin Pudding	Page 106
Pumpkin Rum Punch	Page 107
Pumpkin Sage Muffins	Page 108

Pumpkin Smoothie_____Page 109
Pumpkin Soup_____Page 110
Pumpkin Spice Coffee Creamer_____Page 111
Spiced Pumpkin Seeds_____Page 112

APPLE RECIPES_____Page 113
Apple Cider Shandy_____Page 115
Apple Crisp_____Page 116
Apple Glazed Carrots_____Page 117
Apple Mint Iced Tea_____Page 118
Apple Raisin Chutney_____Page 119
Apple Salad_____Page 120
Applesauce Brownies_____Page 121
Apples & Yams_____Page 122
Baked Apple_____Page 123
Baked Brie & Apples_____Page 124
Barbecue Sauce_____Page 125
Beef Stew_____Page 126
Caramel Apple Cider_____Page 127
Chops and Apples_____Page 128
Cinnamon Apples_____Page 129
Fruit Kabob_____Page 130
Homemade Applesauce_____Page 131
Hot Apple Cranberry Cider_____Page 132
Meatloaf_____Page 133
Pear and Apple Cider_____Page 134
Pork Chops with Applesauce_____Page 135
Sweet Apple Quick Bread_____Page 136

CRANBERRY RECIPES

AFTER THANKSGIVING TURKEY SANDWICH

2 slices of rye bread, seedless if possible
4 slices of turkey
3 ounces of Brie cheese, thinly sliced
2 tablespoons of cranberry Sauce
1 teaspoon of oil

Heat the oil in a skillet or on a grill. Place the bread on a medium-hot skillet and layer 2 pieces of cheese on each bread slice. Let the cheese melt a little. Layer turkey on one slice of the rye bread and top with cranberry sauce. Bring the 2 slices together and continue to heat until golden brown, about 3 to 4 minutes per sides.

APPLE CIDER CRANBERRY PUNCH

1 gallon of apple cider
2 quarts of instant tea
1 quart of cranberry juice
1 quart of orange juice
2 cinnamon sticks
Cloves (to taste)

Combine all ingredients in a large pot and simmer for 10 minutes. Remove cloves and cinnamon sticks and serve warm.

APPLE CRANBERRY FLUFF

2 cups of fresh cranberries, coarsely chopped
2 cups of unpeeled apple, diced
3 cups of miniature marshmallows
1 cup of pineapple, diced and drained
1 cup of whipping cream
½ cup of seeded grapes, drained
½ cup of pecans, coarsely chopped (optional)
¾ cup of sugar
¼ cup of mayonnaise

Mix cranberries, marshmallows and sugar together in a bowl. Cover the bowl and put in the refrigerator overnight. The next day stir in apples, grapes, pineapple and pecans. Whip the cream and fold into the mayonnaise. Slowly fold the cream mixture into the fruit. Chill and serve.

APPLE CRANBERRY PORK CHOPS

4 boneless pork chops
16 ounces of whole cranberry sauce
¾ cup of applesauce

Put the pork chops in a greased slow cooker. Spread the cranberry sauce over the chops and top with the applesauce. Cover the slow cooker and cook on low heat for 6 to 8 hours.

BANANA CRANBERRY BREAD

2 cups of flour
1 cup of sugar
1 cup of ripe banana, mashed
1 cup of pecans, chopped (optional)
½ cup of cranberries, ground and drained
¼ cup of butter
¼ cup of milk
1 egg
3 teaspoons of baking powder
1 teaspoon of lemon or orange rind, grated
½ teaspoon of salt
½ teaspoon of cinnamon

In a large bowl, cream the butter and sugar together. Add the egg into the mixture and beat well. Add the dry ingredients and mix. Alternate small amounts of banana, milk and grated citrus peel into the bowl. Stir until well-mixed. Stir in the cranberries and the pecans. Continue to stir until you have a consistent batter. Pour into a greased and floured loaf pan. Bake at 350 degrees for 60 to 65 minutes.

BEEF TENDERLOIN

2 pounds of beef tenderloin, center-cut
¼ cup of shallots, minced
2 cloves of garlic, minced
1 cup of red wine
1 cup of cranberry juice cocktail
¾ cup of beef broth
3 tablespoon of butter
1 tablespoon of olive oil
1 teaspoon of fresh thyme
Salt and pepper

In a skillet, heat oil and brown the meat on all sides. Place the meat on an oiled baking sheet with a lip. Sprinkle meat with salt and pepper. Save drippings from the skillet. Bake the beef at 425 degrees for 20 to 25 minutes. Loosely cover the meat and let rest for 10 minutes. With the drippings in the skillet, add a tablespoon of butter over cook over medium heat. Add shallots and cook for 1 minute. Stir in garlic and cook for 25 seconds. Pour in the wine and raise the heat to high. Now pour in cranberry juice, beef broth and thyme. Boil the mixture for 10 to 15 minutes or until it thickens slightly. Reduce the heat and stir in remaining butter until it melts. Strain the gravy and serve with meat.

BOG PUNCH

2 quarts of cranberry juice
2 cups of lemon-lime soda (Sprite, 7-Up, etc.)
1 cup of orange juice
1 orange, thinly sliced
1 lime, thinly sliced

Place fruit slices on the bottom of a punch bowl. Mix remaining ingredients together in a separate container then pour over fruit.

CHEESE AND CRANBERRY COOKIES

16 ounces of whole cranberry sauce, canned
2 cups of flour, sifted
2 cups of American cheese, grated
½ cup of butter
¼ cup of milk
½ teaspoon of salt

Mix flour, cheese and salt thoroughly then cut in the butter. Stir in the milk. Roll the dough in foil and chill for a few hours in the refrigerator. Roll the dough out thin on a floured surface. Cut the dough into squares. Spread half of the squares with the cranberry sauce topping with the remaining squares. This forms a cranberry sandwich. Crimp the edges with a fork. Place on an greased cookie sheet and bake at 400 degrees for 10 minutes.

CHICKEN BREAST WITH CRANBERRIES

3 boneless, skinless chicken breasts, cut in half
1 cup of cranberries, fresh or frozen
1 cup of water
¾ cup of flour
½ cup of brown sugar, packed
¼ cup of butter
1 tablespoon of red wine vinegar
½ teaspoon of salt
¼ teaspoon of pepper
Pinch of nutmeg

Combine flour, salt and pepper together thoroughly then dredge chicken pieces in the mix. In a skillet, cook the chicken in the butter until browned on both sides then remove from skillet. In the skillet, combine water, cranberries, brown sugar and nutmeg with the drippings. Cover the skillet and simmer for 5 minutes. Return chicken to the skillet and set on top of the mixture. Cover and simmer on low for 30 minutes. When serving, use the sauce to top the chicken or on the side.

COCKTAIL SAUSAGES

    2 pounds of small smoked sausages
    1 cup of chili sauce
    1 cup of barbecue sauce
    ¾ cup of jellied cranberry sauce

Put sausages in a greased slow cooker. Thoroughly mix chili sauce, barbecue sauce and cranberry sauce and pour over the sausages. Cover and cook on low for 2 to 3 hours.

CRANBERRY ALMOND BREAD

8 ounces of whole berry cranberry sauce
2 cups of flour
1 cup of sugar
1 cup of plain yogurt
½ cup of almonds, chopped
2 eggs
¼ cup of butter
1 teaspoon of almond extract
1 teaspoon of baking soda
½ teaspoon of salt

In a bowl combine flour, baking soda and salt thoroughly. In a second bowl cream butter, sugar and eggs together. Stir in almond extract to the wet mixture. Now alternate adding the flour mixture and the yogurt to the wet mixture and stir thoroughly. Pour half of the batter into a greased and floured loaf pan. Add half of the cranberry sauce and nuts to the pan and swirl lightly throughout the batter. Pour the remaining batter on top and repeat process with remaining cranberry sauce and nuts. Bake at 350 degrees for 1 hour. Let cool for 15 minutes.

CRANBERRY APPLESAUCE

1 can of jellied cranberry sauce
½ cup of applesauce
¼ teaspoon of cinnamon

Combine all ingredients thoroughly and chill for 3 hours.

CRANBERRY BARS

16 ounces of whole cranberry sauce
1½ cups of all-purpose flour
1½ cups of quick-cooking rolled oats
¾ cup of packed brown sugar
1 teaspoon of lemon peel, finely shredded
¼ teaspoon of baking soda
¾ cup of butter, melted
¼ cup of pecans or walnuts, finely chopped

In a large bowl combine flour, oats, brown sugar, lemon peel and baking soda. Stir in butter and mix thoroughly. Reserve 1 cup of this mixture and set aside. Press the remaining mixture in a baking pan. Bake at 350 degrees for 20 minutes. Spread cranberry sauce on top of the baked crust. Combine nuts with the reserved cup of oat mixture and sprinkle on top of the cranberry sauce. Lightly press oat mixture into the sauce. Bake for an additional 25 to 30 minutes more or until top turns golden brown. Remove from oven and let cool then cut into bars.

CRANBERRY BREAD

1 cup of chopped cranberries, fresh or frozen
2 cups of flour
¾ cup of sugar
¾ cup of orange juice
½ cup of nuts, chopped
1 egg, beaten
2 tablespoons of oil
1½ teaspoons of baking powder
½ teaspoon of baking soda
1 teaspoon of salt

Sift all of the dry ingredients together. Stir the cranberries and nuts into the dry ingredients. Add in the remaining ingredients and mix until thoroughly moistened. Lightly grease a loaf pan and fill with the batter. Bake at 350 degrees for 50 minutes.

CRANBERRY BREAD II

2 cups of flour
1 cup of sugar
1 cup of cranberries, diced
1 cup of nuts, chopped
½ cup of orange
3 tablespoons of oil
2 tablespoons of hot water
1½ teaspoons of baking soda
1½ teaspoons of baking powder
1 teaspoon of vanilla
1 egg, beaten
Rind from 1 orange

Mix all of the ingredients together thoroughly. Pour mixture into a greased loaf pan. Bake at 325 degrees for 70 minutes. Remove from pan and let cool.

CRANBERRY CAKE

2 cups of fresh cranberries, cut in half
2 cups of flour
1 cup + 2 tablespoons of sugar
¾ cup of pecans
1/3 cup of orange juice
¼ cup of water
2 tablespoons of butter, melted
1 tablespoon of orange rind, grated
1 egg
1 teaspoon of salt
¾ teaspoon of baking powder
½ teaspoon of baking soda

Mix flour, sugar, salt baking soda and baking powder thoroughly. To this dry mix stir in egg, orange juice, water and butter. Stir just a little keeping the batter thick. Fold in cranberries, pecans and grated orange rind. Pour batter into a greased and floured 8-inch by 8-inch baking pan. Bake at 350 degrees for 40 to 45 minutes.

CRANBERRY CARROTS

10 cups of shredded carrots, loosely packed
1 ½ cups of cranberries, diced large
¼ cup of butter, hard but diced small
¼ cup of sugar
¼ cup of lemon juice
½ teaspoon of salt

Put all of the ingredients in a large baking dish and mix. Cover the dish and bake at 350 for 1 hour or until carrots are tender. Stir a few times during the baking.

CRANBERRY CHICKEN

1 chicken, in pieces
1 package of dry onion soup mix
15 ounces of cranberry sauce or
 canned berries
12 ounces of French dressing

Place the chicken pieces in a lightly greased baking dish. Mix remaining ingredients together and pour over chicken pieces. Bake at 350 degrees for 55 to 65 minutes.

CRANBERRY CITRUS HOLIDAY PUNCH

32 ounces of cranberry juice cocktail
32 ounces of ginger ale
2 cups of orange juice
½ cup of lemon juice
½ cup of honey
¼ cup of lime juice
3 whole cloves
2 cinnamon sticks, crushed

In a large pot, combine all of the ingredients except ginger ale. Simmer over medium heat for 15 minutes. Remove spices. Just before serving pour in the ginger ale and heat thoroughly.

CRANBERRY CHUTNEY

1 cup of cranberries
1 onion, sliced in quarters
1 green pepper, sliced in quarters
1 apple, peeled, cored and quartered
½ cup of sugar
½ cup of apple cider vinegar
¾ teaspoon of salt

Put cranberries, onion, green pepper and apple in a blender or food processor. Chop coarsely. In a pan, combine cranberry mixture with sugar, vinegar and salt. Bring to a boil, reduce heat, cover and simmer for 10 minutes. Cool and refrigerate.

CRANBERRY CONSERVE

1 pound of fresh cranberries
1½ pounds of sugar
1 cup of water
¼ pound of raisins
¼ pound of walnut pieces
1 orange, diced large

In a large pot cook the cranberries, sugar and water until the berries are tender, about 8 minutes. Add raisins, stir and continue to cook for 10 minutes. Add in the orange pieces and walnut pieces, stir and cook for 5 to 10 minutes until mixture thickens. Pour into hot, sterile jars and seal.

CRANBERRY COOLER

4 cups of cranberry juice
4 cups of pineapple juice
1½ cups of sugar
2 liter bottle of ginger ale

Combine cranberry juice, pineapple juice and sugar. Stir until sugar dissolves and refrigerate. Just before serving pour in the ginger ale.

CRANBERRY CRISP

1 can of cranberry sauce
1 cup of oats, quick cooking
1 cup of brown sugar
½ cup of butter
½ cup of flour

Thoroughly mix flour, oats, brown sugar and butter. Spread ¼ of the mixture in a greased baking pan. Spread cranberry sauce over the mixture evenly. Spread remaining oat mixture evenly over the cranberry sauce. Bake at 350 degrees for 45 minutes.

CRANBERRY CURRANT WALNUT SAUCE

1 pound of fresh cranberries
1 cup of sugar
1 cup of red currant jelly
1 cup of orange juice
1 cup of walnuts, finely chopped

Wash the cranberries. In a large pan, mix cranberries, sugar, jelly and orange juice. Stir the mixture and bring to a boil. Reduce the heat and simmer for 20 minutes. Skim any foam that forms on the surface. Remove from heat and stir in the diced walnuts. This sauce is excellent with pork dishes.

CRANBERRY FROST

6 ounces of cream cheese
2 tablespoons of sugar
2 tablespoons of mayonnaise
16 ounces of whole berry cranberry sauce
20 ounces of crushed pineapple
½ cup of pecans, chopped
½ cup of whipped heavy whipping cream

Blend the cream and sugar thoroughly. Stir in the mayonnaise and fold in the rest of the ingredients. Spoon mixture into cupcake papers or into cupcake tins and freeze overnight. Makes about a dozen and a half servings.

CRANBERRY HAM GLAZE

16 ounces of whole cranberry sauce, canned
1 cup of rose wine
1 tablespoons of orange marmalade
4 teaspoons of cornstarch
1½ teaspoons of cinnamon
1¼ cups of firmly packed brown sugar
  or honey

Combine all ingredients in a glass casserole or baking dish. Stir to thoroughly mix. Cook in a microwave oven on high for 5 to 6 minutes or until thickened and bubbly. Baste the ham with the glaze frequently during baking. Serve glaze on the side with ham.

CRANBERRY HONEY RELISH

4 cups of fresh cranberries
1 unpeeled navel orange, cut into large pieces
1 cup of golden raisins
½ cup of honey
½ cup of walnuts or pecans, finely chopped
2 tablespoons of sugar
½ teaspoon of ground ginger
½ teaspoon of ground cinnamon
Pinch of allspice

Grind cranberries and orange together. Do not use a food processor or blender. Combine remaining ingredients thoroughly. Place in a covered container and refrigerate.

CRANBERRY ORANGE PANCAKE SYRUP

1 cup of cranberries, fresh or frozen
¾ cup of orange juice
½ cup of sugar
3 tablespoons of maple syrup

In a pan, add cranberries, orange juice and sugar. Stir thoroughly and bring the mixture to a boil. Reduce the heat and simmer for 5 minutes. Let cool for a few minutes and remove ¼ cup of the cranberries and set aside. Pour the mixture into a blender or food processor and blend until smooth. Pour into a bowl and stir in the ¼ cup of cranberries you set aside and the maple syrup. Keep warm and serve with pancakes.

CRANBERRY PECAN MUFFINS

2 cups of flour
1 cup of sugar
1 cup of sour cream
¾ cup of cranberries, cut in half
½ cup of butter
¼ of pecans, chopped
2 eggs
2 tablespoons of sugar
1 teaspoon of vanilla
1 teaspoon of baking powder
½ teaspoon of baking soda
½ teaspoon of nutmeg
¼ teaspoon of salt
Pinch of nutmeg

Cream butter and slowly add 1 cup of sugar. Beat until mixture is light and fluffy. Fold in sour cream to the mixture. In a bowl, mix flour, baking powder, baking soda, nutmeg and salt. Gradually blend this dry mixture into the butter mixture. Fold in cranberries and nuts and mix. Fill paper muffin cups half-full with batter. Combine remaining 2 tablespoons of sugar with nutmeg and sprinkle over muffins. Bake at 400 degrees for 20 to 25 minutes or until a toothpick tests clean.

CRANBERRY PIE

2 cups of fresh cranberries
1 cup of sugar
1 egg, beaten
½ cup of nuts, chopped
½ cup of flour
¼ cup of melted butter

Combine cranberries, nuts and ½ cup of sugar. Stir thoroughly and pour into a pie pan. Now thoroughly mix beaten egg with ½ cup of sugar, flour and butter. Pour this over the top of the contents in the pie pan. Bake at 300 degrees for 40 to 50 minutes.

CRANBERRY PUDDING

2 cups of whole cranberries
1 1/3 cups of flour
½ cup of chopped nuts
½ cup of dark molasses
1/3 cup of boiling water
2 teaspoons of baking soda
½ teaspoon of salt

Butter Sauce:
1 cup of confectioner's sugar
½ cup of butter
½ cup of evaporated milk
1 teaspoon of vanilla

Mix flour and salt. Dissolve baking soda in boiling water. Combine flour and soda mixtures with molasses and blend completely. Fold in cranberries and nuts. Pour into a greased, floured baking pan and cover. Pour ½ cup of water into a large crockpot or electric roaster. Place covered baking pan into the unit and steam on high for 3 to 4 hours. Pudding will test clean with a toothpick when done. Remove pan and let stand for 5 minutes. Un-mold pudding. For sauce mix ingredients in a pan. Cook over medium heat while stirring. When sugar dissolves and sauce is warm it's ready to serve on pudding.

CRANBERRY RELISH

1 pound of cranberries
1 orange, freshly ground
1 pound of sugar

Grind the orange with the rind. In a bowl mix the orange with cranberry and sugar until sugar dissolves. Let stand overnight. Stir thoroughly again and pack in sterilized jars.

CRANBERRY ROAST

- 3 pound beef chuck roast
- 16 ounces of jellied cranberry sauce, canned
- 1 envelope of dry onion soup mix
- 2 tablespoons of butter
- 2 tablespoons of flour

Pour dry onion soup in the bottom of a slow cooker. Place roast on top of the soup mix and cover the meat with the cranberry sauce. Put the lid on the cooker and set heat on low. Cook for 8 hours. Remove meat from the cooker and raise heat to high. Mix together butter and flour and slowly combine with the liquid in the bottom of the slow cooker to make gravy. Serve gravy with the roast.

CRANBERRY SALAD

1 package of orange Jell-O
1 package of lemon Jell-O
2 cups of boiling water
16 ounces of whole cranberry sauce
¾ cup of pineapple, crushed
1 can of mandarin oranges
Pecans (optional)

Mix ingredients together thoroughly in a bowl. Refrigerate until salad sets.

CRANBERRY TEA

1 pound of fresh cranberries
3 quarts of water
Juice from 3 lemons
Juice from 1 orange
2½ cups of sugar
2 cinnamon sticks
1 teaspoon of whole cloves

Boil cranberries in a large pot with water until the berries pop. Add in remaining ingredients and simmer for 30 minutes. Strain and serve hot.

CRANBERRY WALNUT SAUCE

    2 pounds of cranberries
    1 cup of dried black walnuts. Chopped
    1 cup of maple sugar
    1 cup of cider

Combine all of the ingredients in a pot. Bring the mixture to a boil. Cover the pot and reduce the heat to a simmer for 30 minutes or when the cranberry skins pop.

FRESH CRANBERRY SALAD

1 pound of fresh cranberries, washed
1½ cups of sugar
14 ounces of crushed pineapple, drained
6 ounces of mini-marshmallows
1 cup of nuts, chopped
½ pint of unsweetened whipping cream, whipped

Grind the cranberries; add sugar, stir and cover. Refrigerate the mixture overnight. The next day add pineapple, marshmallows and nuts. Fold in the whipped cream. Chill again before serving.

GORP

Raisins
Dried Cranberries
Dry roasted peanuts or almonds
Sunflower seeds, shelled
Rolled Oats
M&Ms, carob, chocolate or vanilla chips

Mix equal parts of each ingredient and store in a sealed container or plastic bag.

GRANDMA'S CRANBERRY SAUCE

12 ounces of cranberries, fresh or frozen
½ cup of brown sugar
½ cup of sugar
½ cup of orange juice
½ cup of water
¼ teaspoon of cinnamon

In a pan mix water, orange juice, both sugars and cinnamon and stir to dissolve. Once thoroughly mixed, pour in the cranberries. Bring to a boil then reduce to medium heat and cook for 10 minutes or until the berries pop. Mash cranberries in the liquid to help thicken the sauce. Reduce the heat to low and simmer for 10 minutes. Remove the sauce from the heat and refrigerate until serving.

GRILLED CHEESE CRANBERRY SANDWICH

Cheddar cheese, grated
Cranberries, fresh and coarsely chopped
2 slices of bread, thick or dense if possible
Butter
Dijon mustard or honey mustard, optional

Mix grated cheese and cranberries together. Spread butter on both sides of the slices. Spread the mixture on 1 slice of bread and choice of mustard on the other (optional). Close up the sandwich and grill on a medium-hot griddle or skillet. Sandwich is done when bread turns golden brown, about 4 minutes per side.

HONEY PEAR CRANBERRY SAUCE

12 ounces f cranberries, fresh or frozen
2 pears, peeled, cored and diced
1 cup of honey
½ cup of water
½ cup of sugar
1 tablespoon of lemon juice, fresh
1 teaspoon of lemon zest, grated

In a pan combine water and sugar and bring to a boil over medium-high heat. Add diced pears and reduce heat to medium. Cook and stir for 3 minutes then add in cranberries and honey. Cook the mixture for about 5 minutes or until it thickens and the cranberries pop. Remove from heat and stir in lemon juice and lemon zest. Let cool, cover and refrigerate until serving.

HOT CRANBERRY AUTUMN PUNCH

    4 cups of unsweetened pineapple juice
    4 cups of cranberry juice
    ½ cup of packed brown sugar
    1 cup of water
    1 teaspoon of whole cloves
    1 cinnamon stick, crushed
    Vodka to taste (optional)

Combine cloves and cinnamon in a piece of cheesecloth and tie it into a small bag. Combine all of the ingredients in a slow cooker except the vodka. Cook on low for 5 to 8 hours. Remove cheesecloth bag. Add vodka just before serving (optional).

ILWACO CRANBERRY SALAD

2 cups of fresh cranberries
2 cups of unpeeled apples, diced
3 cups of miniature marshmallows
1 cup of whipping cream, whipped
¾ cup of sugar
½ cup of seedless grapes
½ cup of walnuts, coarsely chopped
½ teaspoon of salt

Grind the cranberries and combine with sugar and marshmallows. Cover and chill in the refrigerator overnight. Add apples, grapes, walnuts and salt. Fold in the whipped cream and chill for 3 hours.

ORANGE & GINGER CRANBERRIES

    16 ounces of fresh cranberries
    2 cups of sugar
    1 cup of fresh squeezed orange juice
    1 tablespoon of orange zest
    1 tablespoon of ginger, fresh chopped

Mix all ingredients in a pan and heat until the berries pop open, about 10 to 12 minutes. Cool and refrigerate.

PENINSULA TRAIL MIX

½ cup of banana chips
1 cup of Rice Chex
¼ cup of chocolate or vanilla chips
½ cup of raisins or craisins
1 cup of mini pretzels
1 cup of Cheerios
¼ cup of dried cranberries
¼ cup of cashews
¼ cup of almond slivers
½ cup of dried apple

Put all of the ingredients in a paper bag and shake thoroughly. Pour into a bowl and serve or store in a Ziploc bag for hiking. Measurements are just an example adjust for taste.

PORK CHOPS

4 pork chops, ¾-inch thick
1 tablespoon of oil
¼ teaspoon of salt
Pepper to taste
8 ounces of pineapple slices, canned
½ cup of hot water
½ cup of whole berry cranberry sauce
1 chicken bouillon cube
2 tablespoons of brown sugar
2 tablespoons of vinegar
1 sweet pepper, cut into rings

In a skillet, brown the pork chops in the oil. Sprinkle chops with salt and pepper. Drain the juice from the pineapple, saving the liquid. Mix the juice with ½ cup of hot water, the cranberry sauce, bouillon cube, brown sugar and vinegar. Pour this over the chops, cover and simmer for 20 minutes. Top the chops with the pineapple and pepper rings, cover and simmer for 10 more minutes.

PORK TENDERLOIN

1 pound pork tenderloin
14 ounces of whole cranberry sauce
½ cup of orange juice
¼ cup of sugar
2 tablespoons of cornstarch
3 tablespoons of cold water
1 tablespoon of brown sugar
1 teaspoon of ground mustard
¼ teaspoon of ground cloves

Place the pork in a slow cooker. In a bowl combine cranberry sauce, orange juice, sugars, mustard and cloves and pour over the pork. Cover and cook on low for 5 to 6 hours or until meat is tender. Remove pork but keep it warm. Combine cornstarch with cold water and stir until smooth. Gradually stir into the cranberry mixture. Cover and cook for 15 minutes or until thickened. Serve sauce with pork.

SIMPLE CRANBERRY SAUCE

12 ounces of cranberries, fresh or frozen
1 cup of sugar
1 cup of water

Mix water and sugar in a pan and bring to a boil. Stir in the cranberries and bring to a boil again. Reduce heat to a light boil for 10 minutes and stir ever minute. Cover and let cool completely. Keep in the refrigerator until mealtime.

SLOW COOKED TURKEY BREAST

3 pound boneless turkey breast
16 ounces of cranberry sauce
½ cup of orange juice
1 envelope of dry onion soup mix

Mash the cranberry sauce in a bowl and mix thoroughly with dry onion soup mix and orange juice. Spay the slow cooker or crock pot with cooking spray and put the turkey breast inside the cooker. Pour the sauce over the turkey breast. Set the cooker on low heat and cook until tender, about 7 to 8 hours.

SPICED CRANBERRY TEA

1 quart of apple cider
3 cups of strong tea
12 ounces of frozen concentrated cranberry juice
6 inch cinnamon stick, broken into pieces
1 cup of water
¼ cup of sugar
2 teaspoons of whole cloves

Place the cinnamon stick pieces and cloves in a double-thickness of cheesecloth. Bring up the corners and tie with a string. In a large pan or crock-pot mix sugar and water. Heat until sugar dissolves. Add spice bag, cranberry juice, cider and tea. Cover and heat but do not boil. Remove spice bag. When pouring into mugs garnish with a candy cane.

SPICY CRANBERRY CHUTNEY

4 cups of fresh cranberries
1 cup of seedless raisins
1 cup of water
1 onion, diced
1 apple, pared and diced
1¾ cups of sugar
½ cup of celery, thinly sliced
1½ teaspoons of ginger
1 tablespoon of cinnamon
¼ teaspoon of cloves

Mix cranberries, raisins, sugar, cinnamon, ginger, cloves and water in a pan. Simmer for 15 minutes until the berries pop and the mixture thickens. Stir in onion, apple and celery. Simmer for 15 minutes or until mixture thickens. Cool and refrigerate.

TANGY CRANBERRY SAUCE

12 ounces of fresh cranberries
2 cups of sugar
1 cup of orange juice
  (fresh squeezed if possible)
1 tablespoons of fresh grated ginger root
1 tablespoon of orange zest

After washing the berries, put all ingredients in a pan. Bring to a boil the reduce heat and simmer for 15 minutes. Cool and serve. Leftover can store in the refrigerator up to 2 weeks.

TURKEY BREAST

4 pound turkey breast
16 ounces of whole cranberry sauce
¼ cup of water
1 package of dry onion and herb soup mix

Place the turkey breast inside a greased slow cooker. Combine remaining ingredients thoroughly and pour over the top of the turkey. Cover and cook on low for 8 to 10 hours.

WHITE CHOCOLATE CRANBERRY COOKIES

1½ cups of diced cranberries, fresh or frozen
1½ cups of sugar
1½ cups of all-purpose flour
1½ cups of quick rolled oats
6 ounces of white chocolate chips
1 cup of butter, room temperature
1 large egg
2 teaspoons of baking soda

Mix butter, sugar and baking soda in a bowl. Blend until it becomes creamy. Beat in an egg then stir in four, oats and white chocolate chips. Add cranberry pieces to the dough. Drop spoonfuls of the dough onto a cookie sheet. Bake at 350 degrees for 10 to 12 minutes.

PUMPKIN RECIPES

AUTUMN SOUP

4 cups of chicken broth
15 ounces of pumpkin, canned
1 cup of celery, diced
½ cup of yellow onion, diced
2 tablespoons of dry white wine
1 tablespoon of butter
1 teaspoon of salt
½ teaspoon of dried sage
Parmesan cheese, grated

In a pot melt the butter and sauté onion and celery for 5 minutes or until tender. Add 1 cup of chicken broth, cover and simmer for 10 minutes. Pour into a food processor or blender and puree until smooth. Return to pot and add remaining ingredients except cheese. Stir and simmer until well blended and thoroughly heated. When serving pour into bowls and sprinkle with Parmesan cheese.

BAKED PUMPKIN

1 small pumpkin
¼ cup of maple syrup
¼ cup of apple cider
¼ cup of melted butter

Place the pumpkin in an oven and bake at 350 degrees for 90 minutes to 2 hours. Cut a hole in the top and scoop out the seeds and the pulp. Set seeds aside for later snacking. Mix together the maple syrup, apple cider and butter thoroughly. Pour into the pumpkin and bake for 35 minutes. Cut into wedges and serve.

BEAN & PUMPKIN SOUP

3 cups of vegetable broth
2 cups of tomatoes, diced
1½ cups of pumpkin, cubed
1 cup of fresh corn
1 cup of dried beans, soaked overnight
1 onion, sliced
1 green pepper, diced
1 clove of garlic, minced
3 tablespoons of fresh oregano, minced
1 tablespoon of chili powder
2 teaspoons of olive oil

Drain the soaked beans and set aside. In a skillet sauté the onion, garlic, oregano and chili powder in oil for 5 minutes. Stir in the diced tomatoes and simmer for 5 minutes. Pour the mixture into a casserole or baking dish. Add the beans and broth to the mixture. Bake at 375 degrees for 90 minutes. Stir in green pepper, pumpkin and corn and bake for 1 hour.

CHICKEN PUMPKIN CHILI

3 cups of chicken broth
2 cups of pumpkin puree
1 pound of boneless, skinless diced chicken
15 ounces of tomatoes, diced
15 ounces of canned garbanzo beans, drained
2 tablespoons of olive oil
1 large yellow onion, diced
1 green bell pepper, diced
2 large carrots, peeled and chopped
4 cloves of garlic, minced
1 tablespoon of ground cumin
1 teaspoon of Cajun seasoning
½ teaspoon of ground sage
½ teaspoon ground cinnamon
Salt to taste

In a pot, heat oil and sauté onion for 3 minutes then add bell pepper and carrot. Sauté vegetables for 8 minutes or until soft but not completely cooked. Stir constantly. Add garlic, cumin, sage, Cajun seasoning and cinnamon. Stir and cook for 1 minute. Add chicken and allow the meat to brown slightly, but do not cook through. Add remaining ingredients and stir thoroughly. Bring to a boil. Reduce heat to medium-low and simmer for 35 minutes or until vegetables and chicken are cooked.

CHOCOLATE CHIP PUMPKIN CAKE

3 cups of flour
2 cups of sugar
2 cups of pumpkin, canned
1 cup of vegetable oil
1 cup of nuts, chopped (optional)
1 package of chocolate chip chips
4 eggs
2 teaspoons of baking soda
2 teaspoons of baking powder
½ teaspoon of salt
½ teaspoon of cinnamon

Grease a Bundt pan. In a bowl, mix all of the ingredients together thoroughly. Pour the batter into the pan. Bake at 350 degrees for 90 minutes.

CREAMY PUMPKIN SOUP

5 cup of pumpkin, cubed
2 cups of vegetable stock
1 cup of milk
1 cup of cream
1 cup of onion, diced
1 teaspoon of butter
¼ teaspoon of nutmeg, freshly grated
Cayenne pepper to taste

In a large pan or pot, sauté onions in the butter until they are translucent. Stir in pumpkin and broth and cook until the pumpkin is soft. Put the mixture into a blender or food processor and puree. Put the mixture back in the pot and add milk and cream. Heat the ingredients thoroughly but do not boil. Season the soup with nutmeg and cayenne a few minutes before removing from the heat.

GINGER PUMPKIN SOUP

1 pound of fresh pumpkin, cubed
2 cups of chicken broth
1 cup of Half & Half
1 small onion, diced
2 tablespoons of fresh ginger, chopped
1 tablespoon of butter
2 teaspoons of curry
1 teaspoon of turmeric
Salt

Melt butter in a pot and sauté onion until tender. Add pumpkin, broth and ginger and cook over medium heat for 15 minutes or until very tender. Puree mixture in a blender until smooth. Return pumpkin mixture to pot and add curry, turmeric and Half & Half. Heat thoroughly without boiling. Salt to taste.

HARVEST PUMPKIN CAKE

1 cup of sugar
1 cup of pumpkin
2 eggs
2/3 cup of flour
1/3 cup of oil
½ cup of brown sugar
½ cup of walnuts, chopped
1 teaspoon of baking soda
½ teaspoon of salt
½ teaspoon of nutmeg
½ teaspoon of cinnamon
¼ teaspoon of cloves
¼ teaspoon of baking powder

Mix the dry ingredients thoroughly. Add pumpkin, eggs, oil and nuts. Pour the batter into a greased and floured baking dish, Bake at 300 degrees for 45 to 55 minutes. Test with a toothpick. If it comes out clean from the center it's done.

HARVEST PUMPKIN PIE

1½ cups of cooked pumpkin
1½ cups of milk
1 cup of brown sugar
½ cup of cream or evaporated milk
2 eggs, slightly beaten
1 tablespoon of angostura bitters
1 teaspoon of cinnamon
½ teaspoon of salt
½ teaspoon of ginger
1 unbaked pie shell

Combine all ingredients and mix thoroughly. Pour into the pie shell. Bake at 425 degrees for 40 to 45 minutes or until a knife inserted in the center comes out clean.

HIDATSA PUMPKIN

1 five-pound sugar pumpkin
2 teaspoons of salt
½ teaspoon of dry mustard
2 tablespoons of vegetable oil or rendered fat
1 pound of ground, venison, buffalo or beef
1 medium onion, diced
1 cup of wild or brown rice, cooked
3 eggs, beaten
1 teaspoon of sage, dried and crushed
¼ teaspoon of pepper

Cut the top off the pumpkin, like you would for a Jack O'Lantern. Remove the seeds and strings. Prick the cavity with a fork all over and rub with 1 teaspoon of salt and the dry mustard throughout. Heat oil in large skillet. Add meat and onion and sauté over medium-high heat until browned. Remove from the heat and stir in wild rice, eggs, remaining salt, sage and pepper. Stuff the pumpkin with this mixture. Place ½-inch of water in the bottom of a shallow baking pan and place the pumpkin with the lid on, in the pan and bake for 90 minutes or until tender. Add more water to the pan as necessary to avoid sticking.

HONEY PUMPKIN BUTTER

2 cups of pureed pumpkin, cooked
½ cup of honey
1 teaspoon of lemon zest, grated
1 tablespoon of fresh lemon juice
1 teaspoon of ground cinnamon
¼ teaspoon of ginger, ground
¼ teaspoon of salt
Pinch of fresh nutmeg, grated
Pinch of ground cloves

In a pan thoroughly mix all of the ingredients. Simmer the mixture uncovered over low heat for 35 minutes or until it becomes thick. When it's done cooking keep in a tightly sealed container in the fridge.

HOT PUMPKIN EGGNOG

2 cups of boiling water
½ cup of pumpkin
2 eggs
2 tablespoons of butter
2 tablespoons of coconut oil
2 tablespoons of honey
1 teaspoon of pumpkin pie spice
½ teaspoon of vanilla extract
¼ teaspoon of sea salt
Fresh ground cinnamon

Pour all but the last ingredient into a blender and blend until smooth. Pour into mugs and sprinkle cinnamon on top.

JACK O' LANTERN SOUP

2 cups of pumpkin puree
2 cups of vegetable broth
1 cup of tomatoes, chopped
1 cup of milk
½ cup of yellow onions, diced
¼ cup of fresh parsley, minced
¼ cup of green peppers, chopped
1 tablespoon of olive oil
1 tablespoon of flour
¼ teaspoon of fresh thyme, minced
Fresh ground pepper
Salt
1 bay leaf

In a large pot, sauté green peppers and onions in olive oil. Sprinkle in flour and stir until lightly browned. Add in pumpkin puree, tomatoes, broth, parsley, thyme and bay leaf. Cover and simmer for 30 while stirring occasionally. Remove the bay leaf and add milk. Season with salt and pepper to taste and heat thoroughly.

MAPLE PUMPKIN CHEESECAKE

1 graham cracker piecrust, 8-inch diameter
1 pound of low-fat cottage cheese
¾ cup of pumpkin puree
½ cup of plain low-fat yogurt
¼ cup of flour
¼ cup of maple syrup
3 eggs
1 teaspoon of vanilla
½ teaspoon of pumpkin pie spice

Alternating between the wet and dry ingredients, slowly put in each item a little at a time into a blender or food processor. Blend until smooth then pour into the piecrust and spread evenly. Bake at 325 degrees for 50 minutes. Let cool before cutting and serving.

NO BAKE PUMPKIN PIE

15 ounces of pumpkin puree
2 cups of ginger snap crumbs, finely crushed
½ cup of milk
¼ cup of butter, melted
7½ ounces of instant vanilla pudding mix
1¼ teaspoons of cinnamon
¾ teaspoon of ground ginger
¼ teaspoon of ground nutmeg

In a pan mix together gingersnap crumbs and butter until the crumbs are coated. Press the crumbs into the bottom and sides of a pie tin. In a bowl whisky pudding mix and milk together until well blended. Stir in pumpkin puree, cinnamon, ginger and nutmeg. Spread the pumpkin mixture evenly in the pie tin. Cover and refrigerate overnight.

ORANGE GINGER PUMPKIN SEEDS

    2 cups of pumpkin seeds
    1 tablespoon of butter
    1 teaspoon of ground ginger
    ½ teaspoon of grated orange zest

Coast the seeds with melted butter and toss with ginger and orange zest. Spread seeds on a baking sheet and bake at 350 degrees for 30 minutes.

PATCH & ORCHARD COCKTAIL

2 ounces of apple cider
1½ ounces of pumpkin puree
1½ ounces of vanilla vodka
1½ ounces of spicy ginger ale (like Vernors)
Ice

Fill a cocktail shaker with ice, pumpkin puree, vanilla vodka and apple cider. Shake for 10 to 15 seconds and strain into a glass and top with the ginger ale.

PUMPKIN BREAD

4 cups of flour
2 cups of fresh pumpkin
1 cup of chopped nuts (optional)
1 cup of oil
1 cup of sugar
1 cup of brown sugar
4 teaspoons of soda
1 teaspoon of salt
1 teaspoon of cloves
1 teaspoon of cinnamon

Mix oil and sugars together, and then combine with pumpkin and nuts. Mix dry ingredients together thoroughly. Combine wet and dry mixtures and blend well. Divide batter into 2 or 3 loaves. Bake at 325 degrees for 45 to 50 minutes.

PUMPKIN BURGER

2 pounds of ground beef
2 cans of pumpkin
1 tablespoon of oil
1 onion, diced
¾ cup of hot water
1 cup of ketchup
½ cup of tomato juice
¼ teaspoon of nutmeg
½ teaspoon of cloves
1 teaspoon of chili powder
1 teaspoon of salt
½ teaspoon of black pepper
8 hamburger buns

Brown ground beef in a skillet with the oil. Add onion and cook for 5 minutes. In a large pan add ketchup, tomato juice, nutmeg, cloves, chili powder, salt and pepper. Bring this mixture to a rolling boil. Add pumpkin, meat and onions to the boiling mixture and simmer for 15 minutes. Scoop onto hamburger buns.

PUMPKIN CANDY

1 5-pound pumpkin
5 cups of sugar
1 tablespoons of baking soda
Water

Peel the pumpkin and remove the seeds. Cut pumpkin into strips of 2-inches by 4 inches. Stir baking soda into enough water to cover the strips in a glass or ceramic baking dish. Soak the strips for 12 hours, drain and wash in cool running water. Drop the strips into a pot of boiling water. Boil the strips until tender but not soft. Remove strips and drop into ice water. Mix sugar with 1 cup of water and boil for 10 minutes to make a syrup. Combine syrup with the strips in a covered put and simmer until the pumpkin is brittle. Remove the strips and let dry on a rack or paper towel.

PUMPKIN CASSEROLE

1½ pounds of fresh pumpkin
1 large onion, chopped fine
½ teaspoon of salt
¼ teaspoon of ground white pepper
2 tablespoons unsalted butter, melted
2 eggs
¾ cup of milk
¾ cup of ricotta cheese

Slice the pumpkin into ¼-inch slices and place in a mixing bowl. Add the onion, salt, pepper and butter and toss. Pour contents of the bowl into a 9-inch greased baking dish, cover with foil and place in the oven. Bake at 375 degrees for 30 minutes. Beat eggs, milk and cheese together until smooth. Remove the baking dish from the oven, remove the cover and pour the cheese mixture over the top. Replace in oven, uncovered and bake for another 20 minutes. When cheese turns golden brown it's done.

PUMPKIN CHAI TEA LATTE

- 1 cup of prepared sweetened Chai tea concentrate
- 1 cup of milk
- ¼ cup of pumpkin puree
- ½ teaspoon of vanilla
- ¼ teaspoon of cinnamon

In a pan combine Chai tea concentrate, milk, pumpkin puree and vanilla. Cook over medium heat until it reaches a simmer. Whisk while heating. Sample the flavor. Add more milk if needed. Strain puree from the tea if you would like. Pour into mugs and sprinkle with cinnamon.

PUMPKIN CORNBREAD

1 cup of pumpkin puree
1 cup of flour
1 cup of cornmeal
½ cup of brown sugar, packed
1/3 cup of vegetable oil
1/3 cup of buttermilk
2 eggs
2 tablespoons of molasses
1 tablespoon of baking powder
1 teaspoon of salt
½ teaspoon of ground ginger or cinnamon
¼ teaspoon of ground nutmeg

In a bowl thoroughly mix the dry ingredients. In a second bowl thoroughly mix all of the wet ingredients. Combine wet and dry ingredients into a consistent batter. Pour batter into a greased 8-inch by 8-inch baking pan. Bake at 400 degrees for 30 to 35 minutes or when a toothpick tests clean from the center.

PUMPKIN FUDGE

3 cups of sugar
12 ounces of white chocolate morsels
7 ounces of marshmallow crème
1 cup of chopped pecans, toasted (optional)
¾ cup of melted butter
2/3 cup of evaporated milk
½ cup of canned pumpkin
2 tablespoons of corn syrup
1 teaspoon of pumpkin pie spice
1 teaspoon of vanilla extract

Stir together sugar, butter, milk, pumpkin, corn syrup and pie spice in a saucepan over medium-high heat, and cook, stirring constantly, until mixture comes to a boil. Cook, stirring constantly, until a candy thermometer registers 234° (soft-ball stage) or for about 12 minutes. Remove the pan from the heat; stir in remaining ingredients until thoroughly mixed. Pour the batter into a greased and foil-lined 9-inch by 9-inch baking pan. Let the fudge stand until completely cool then cut the fudge into squares.

PUMPKIN GRANOLA

2½ cups of rolled oats
¾ cup of dried cranberries
1/3 cup toasted pumpkin seeds
1/3 cup toasted pecans, chopped
1/3 cup of brown sugar
1/3 cup of pumpkin puree
¼ cup of applesauce
2 tablespoons of maple syrup
¾ teaspoon of pumpkin pie spice
½ teaspoon of cinnamon
¼ teaspoon of nutmeg
¼ teaspoon of salt
½ teaspoon of vanilla extract

Line a baking sheet with parchment paper. In a bowl combine oats, spices, salt and mix. In a second bowl, mix brown sugar, pumpkin puree, applesauce, maple syrup and vanilla extract. Whisk until smooth. Combine both mixtures and stir until the oats are coated. Spread mixture onto baking sheet. Bake at 325 degrees for 20 minutes. Stir granola. Bake for an additional 20 minutes or until the granola is crisp and golden. Add pumpkin seeds and pecans to the pan in the last 4 minutes of baking. After removing from oven add dried cranberries and let cool.

PUMPKIN HICKORY CAKE

2 cups of cornmeal, ground fine
1½ cups of stewed pumpkin, blended smooth
1 cup of potato flour
½ cup of maple syrup
¼ cup of dried hickory nuts,
   shelled and chopped
1 egg, beaten
1 teaspoon of water

In a bowl combine cornmeal and potato flour. Beat the egg with 1 tablespoon of water. Gradually blend all of the ingredients into the flour mixture until you have a smooth batter. Pour into a well-greased loaf pan and bake at 350 degrees for 75 minutes.

PUMPKIN HUMMUS

1 cup of chickpeas, skins removed
¾ cup of canned pumpkin
¼ cup of maple syrup
2 teaspoons of pumpkin pie spice
2 teaspoons of coconut oil, melted

Mix all 5 ingredients together in a food processor or blender until smooth. Pour and scrape the hummus into a bowl, Drizzle with additional coconut oil if you like. Serve or chill before serving.

PUMPKIN MEATLOAF

4 pounds of ground beef
4 ounces of breadcrumbs
1 cup of canned pumpkin
2 eggs
1 teaspoon of kosher salt
1 teaspoon of cinnamon
1 teaspoon of chili powder
1 clove of garlic
½ teaspoon of paprika (optional)
Barbecue sauce of choice (optional)

Combine all ingredients, except the barbecue sauce, thoroughly. Push the mixture into a lightly greased loaf pan. Bake at 400 degrees for 75 minutes or until internal loaf temperature reaches 160 degrees. Just before cutting and serving, warm the barbecue sauce and pour over the loaf.

PUMPKIN MUFFINS

15 ounces of pure pumpkin puree
1¾ cups of all-purpose flour
1 cup of sugar
½ cup of dark brown sugar
½ cup of coconut oil, melted
2 eggs
2 teaspoons of cinnamon
1 teaspoon of vanilla extract
1 teaspoon of baking soda
½ teaspoon of salt
¼ teaspoon of ground cloves
¼ teaspoon of nutmeg

Put 12 paper liners into each well of your standard size muffin pan. Measure out the flour, sugars, baking soda, salt and spices in a medium bowl and whisk together. Set aside. In a second bowl, whisk together eggs, pumpkin puree, coconut oil and vanilla extract. Pour the wet ingredients into the dry ingredients and stir together. Do not over mix, just stir until everything is mixed into the batter. Scoop the batter into each muffin liner. They should be almost full. Bake muffins at 375 degrees for 20 to 22 minutes or until a toothpick inserted into the center of a muffin comes out clean.

PUMPKIN MUSHROOM SOUP

16 ounces of pumpkin, canned
14 ounces of chicken broth
1 cup of water
½ cup of whole milk or Half & Half
½ cup of onion, diced
½ cup of celery, diced
¼ cup of shitake mushrooms, dried
2 tablespoons of butter
Salt and pepper

Soak the mushrooms in the water for 30 minutes. Drain and reserve. Chop the mushrooms, removing the stems. In a pot sauté onion and celery in butter. Stir in mushrooms, reserved water, pumpkin and chicken broth. Cover the pot and cook on medium heat until thoroughly cooked. Season the mixture with salt and pepper. Reduce the heat and stir in milk or Half & Half and heat thoroughly. Do not boil.

PUMPKIN OATMEAL

1 cup of steel cut oats
1 cup of pumpkin puree
3 cups of water
2 teaspoons of vanilla
½ teaspoon of pumpkin pie spice
½ teaspoon of cinnamon
1 teaspoon of sugar or stevia (optional)
1 pinch of salt

Combine all of the ingredients in a bowl and stir thoroughly. Place the bowl in a slow cooker and fill the slow cooker with water until it reaches halfway up the bowl. Cover the cooker and set on low heat for 6 to 8 hours. Top with honey, syrup, brown sugar or fruit of choice.

PUMPKIN PANCAKES

12 ounces of nonfat evaporated milk, unsweetened
1 cup of unbleached white flour
1 cup of pumpkin, canned
½ cup of whole-wheat flour
1 egg
1 tablespoon of baking powder
½ teaspoon of cinnamon
½ teaspoon of salt
½ teaspoon of vanilla extract
¼ teaspoon of nutmeg

In a bowl sift flours, baking powder, salt, cinnamon and nutmeg together. In a second, bowl whisk milk, pumpkin, egg and vanilla together. Combine the wet and dry ingredients until you have a moist batter. On a lightly oil hot griddle or skillet, pour batter, about ¼-cup per pancake. When the bubbles on the pancake start to burst, flip and grill until golden brown.

PUMPKIN PICKLES

1 sugar pumpkin, 3 to 4 pounds
5 cups of sugar
3 cups of cider vinegar
¼ cup of fresh ginger, fresh & finely chopped
20 black peppercorns
3 strips of lemon zest
2 cinnamon sticks
1 tablespoon of salt
4 1-pint canning jars

Seed and peel the pumpkin and cut into strips about 2 inches long and ¾ of an inch thick and wide. In a large pan, mix lemon zest, sugar, vinegar, ginger, cinnamon, peppercorns and salt. Simmer and stir for 5 minutes or until sugar is dissolved. Add the pumpkin strips to the mixture. Stir occasionally and cook for 15 minutes until crisp and tender. Transfer pumpkin to sterilized canning jars. Pour in the cooking liquid to within a ¼-inch of the top of each jar. Seal and refrigerate if you plan on eating within the week. For long-term storage follow instructions from canning jar manufacturer.

PUMPKIN PIE

2½ cups of cooked pumpkin
3 eggs, separated
1 cup of brown sugar
1 cup of light cream
¼ cup of butter, melted
1½ teaspoons of cinnamon
½ teaspoon of ginger
½ teaspoon of salt
¼ teaspoon of cloves
1 8-inch unbaked pie shell

Combine pumpkin, sugar, salt, cinnamon, cloves and ginger. Beat egg yolks lightly. Beat egg whites until stiff. Add egg yolks, cream and butter to the pumpkin mixture. Mix thoroughly the fold in the egg whites. Pour mixture into the pie shell. Bake at 450 degrees for 10 minutes. Reduce oven to 350 degrees and bake for 35 minutes or until pie tests done.

PUMPKIN PIE JELL-O SHOTS

15 ounces of pure pumpkin, canned
12 ounces of evaporated milk
12 mini graham cracker piecrusts
2 envelopes of Knox unflavored gelatin
1 cup of vanilla vodka
½ cup of sugar or brown sugar
2 teaspoons of pumpkin pie spice
1 teaspoon of vanilla extract
Whip cream

In a pot, boil the evaporated milk and pour it into the gelatin mixture. Mix well until the gelatin dissolves completely. Add sugar and stir until it dissolves completely. Add the pumpkin pie spice, vanilla extract and pure pumpkin to the gelatin mixture. Stir well until everything is mixed Thoroughly. Pour the mixture into mini graham cracker piecrusts and place them in the refrigerator. Refrigerate the shots for about two hours or until firm. Top with whip cream.

PUMPKIN PIE FRUIT LEATHER

15 ounces of pumpkin puree, canned
1 cup of unsweetened applesauce
1 cup of coconut milk
¼ cup of honey
1 teaspoon of cinnamon
1 teaspoon of nutmeg
½ teaspoon of ground cloves
½ teaspoon of ground ginger
2 tablespoons of fresh squeezed lemon juice
1 teaspoon of coconut oil
Cornstarch

Combine the first 8 ingredients in a blender or food processor. Puree on high until the mixture is smooth. Pour in the lemon juice and blend for 10 more seconds. Line a baking tray with parchment paper and brush with coconut oil. Pour the pumpkin puree on the sheet and smooth until even. The oven should be preheated at 175 degrees. Place the tray inside the oven, leaving the door open slightly for moisture to escape. Bake for 8 to 12 hours. The fruit leather should be soft but no mushy, chewy but not hard. If you're using a food dehydrator bake 5 to 8 hours depending on make, model and power. When baking is finished, cut into strips and dust with cornstarch.

PUMPKIN PIE MILKSHAKE

1 cup of vanilla ice cream
¾ cup of milk
½ cup of pure pumpkin
¾ teaspoon of pumpkin pie spice

Mix pumpkin, ice cream, milk and pie spice in a blender until smooth. Pour into a tall glass. Top with a sprinkle of pumpkin pie spice (optional).

PUMPKIN PIE POPSICLE

1½ cups of milk (whole or 2%)
1 cup of pumpkin puree, canned
1 box of instant vanilla pudding mix
½ teaspoon of ginger
¼ teaspoon of nutmeg
¼ teaspoon of cinnamon
¼ teaspoon of allspice
¼ teaspoon pf cloves
¼ teaspoon of cardamom

Whisk ingredients together until smooth. Fill the popsicle molds to the top. Position the sticks in the center of each pop. If needed, cover the top with plastic wrap and poke stick through into the mold. The wrap will hold the sticks until the popsicles begin to freeze. Put the popsicles in the refrigerator for at least 6 hours. To remove, hold the popsicle mold in hot water until they release.

PUMPKIN PINE NUT BREAD

2 cups of flour
2 cups of cooked pumpkin
1½ cups of pine nuts, roasted
1½ cups of sugar
¾ cup of milk
½ cup of oil
3 eggs, beaten
1 teaspoon of baking soda
1 teaspoon of vanilla
½ teaspoon of salt

To roast the pine nuts, spread them on an ungreased cookie sheet and bake at 375 degrees for 10 minutes. In a bowl mix the flour, baking soda, salt and sugar together thoroughly. In a second bowl, combine eggs, milk, oil and vanilla. Mix thoroughly and stir in the pumpkin. Stir in the dry ingredients and mix thoroughly. Stir in the roasted pine nuts. Pour the batter into 2 greased loaf pans. Bake at 350 degrees for 40 to 45 minutes.

PUMPKIN PUDDING

3 eggs, lightly beaten
2½ cups of rich milk
2 cups of pumpkin
½ teaspoon of lemon extract
1¾ cups of sugar
2 heaping tablespoons of flour
1 teaspoon of salt
1 teaspoon of cinnamon
½ teaspoon of ginger
Pinch of soda

Mix together the first four ingredients then add in the dry ingredients. Mix well and bake at 350 degrees until it tests for doneness.

PUMPKIN RUM PUNCH

1 fifth of dark rum
3 cinnamon sticks
10 ounces of pumpkin puree
10 ounces of sweetened condensed milk
10 dashes of Angostura bitters
Fresh ground nutmeg
Ice cubes

In a large jar, combine rum and cinnamon sticks. Seal and place in a dark place for 3 days. Shake gently each day. In a punch bowl, combine 10 ounces of the cinnamon-infused rum with pumpkin puree, condensed milk and bitters. Stir to mix all of the flavors. Add ice cubes or an ice block. Sprinkle fresh ground nutmeg over the punch.

PUMPKIN SAGE MUFFIN

2½ cups of oats
2 cups of pumpkin puree
1 cup of whole-wheat flour
¼ cup of sage
¼ cup of olive oil
1 tablespoon of apple cider vinegar
1 teaspoon of baking soda
1 teaspoon of baking powder
1 teaspoon of salt

Mix all the dry ingredients till well combined. Chop the sage into small pieces and stir into the dry mixture. Add the pumpkin puree, olive oil and vinegar and stir thoroughly but do not over mix the dough. Scoop batter into a muffin tray and bake at 325 degrees 160 for 30 to 35 minutes or until the toothpick tests clean.

PUMPKIN SMOOTHIE

1 cup of non-unsweetened almond milk
½ cup of canned pumpkin
½ banana
½ teaspoon of maple syrup
½ teaspoon of vanilla extract
¼ teaspoon of ground cinnamon
⅛ teaspoon ground ginger
Pinch of ground nutmeg
Pinch of ground cloves
Pinch of all spice

Drop all of the ingredients into a blender and process until smooth. If you like, drop in some ice cubes while blending.

PUMPKIN SOUP

1 stick of butter
1 onion, coarsely chopped
5 pounds of pumpkin
1 cup of heavy cream
1 quart of water
1 pinch of nutmeg
Salt and pepper

Wash and peel pumpkin and remove seeds. Cut pumpkin into 2-inch cubes. Melt butter in large pot and add onions. Cook the onions until tender. Add pumpkin and water. Season the mixture with salt, pepper and nutmeg. Simmer for 20 to 30 minutes. Puree mixture and add cream. If too thick add water.

PUMPKIN SPICE COFFEE CREAMER

2½ cups of Half & Half
½ cup of canned pumpkin
3 tablespoons of sugar
1½ teaspoons of pumpkin pie spice

Put all of the ingredients in a pan. Set for medium and heat and continue to stir until the Half & Half is hot. Do not let the mixture boil. When thoroughly mixed and heated, pour through a fine strainer. Pour strained liquid into a sealed container and store in the refrigerator.

SPICED PUMPKIN SEEDS

2 cups of raw whole pumpkin seeds
1½ tablespoons of butter, melted
2 teaspoons of Worcestershire sauce
½ teaspoons of salt
Garlic salt to taste

Combine all ingredients in a bowl and mix thoroughly. Spread the seeds and mixture on a baking pan. Bake at 275 degrees for 1 hour. Stir occasionally.

APPLE RECIPES

APPLE CIDER SHANDY

    6 ounces of apple cider
    6 ounces of pumpkin beer
    1 cinnamon stick

Pour cider into a glass, top with the pumpkin beer and add the cinnamon stick.

APPLE CRISP

5 cups of sliced apples
¾ cup of flour
1 teaspoon of cinnamon
1 cup of brown sugar
¾ cup of rolled oats
½ cup of butter

Arrange apples in a buttered pan. Combine sugar, flour, oats and cinnamon. Cut in butter until crumbly. Press over apples. Bake at 350 degrees for about 45 minutes.

APPLE GLAZED CARROTS

16 ounces of baby carrots
¼ cup of apple cider
¼ cup of apple jelly
1 ½ teaspoons of Dijon mustard

Place the carrots and apple cider in a small pan. Bring to a boil then reduce heat. Cover and simmer for 8 minutes or until carrots are tender. Remove cover and cook on medium heat until liquid evaporates the stir in jelly and mustard. Cook until jelly melts and carrots are glazed.

APPLE MINT ICED TEA

    2 cups of apple juice
    1 cup of water
    1 cup of fresh mint leaves, chopped
    7 tea bags of herbal or black tea

In a pot mix water, apple juice and mint leaves and bring to a boil. Add tea bags and steep for 5 minutes. Let cool or chill and serve over ice.

APPLE RAISIN CHUTNEY

2 tart apples, peeled, cored and diced
½ cup of raisins
½ cup of brown sugar
¼ cup of apple cider vinegar
¼ cup of onion, diced
¼ cup of water
1 teaspoon of turmeric
½ teaspoon of ginger
¼ teaspoon of salt
¼ teaspoon of ginger
Cloves to taste

For this recipe, fresh ground spices yield the best results. Combine all ingredients in a pan and cook over medium heat for 20 to 25 minutes. Stir the mixture occasionally. Once it reaches a boil, reduce heat to a simmer. Let the mixture cool and cover. Refrigerate overnight.

APPLE SALAD

2 apples, diced
1 cup of pineapple, crushed or bits
¼ cup of celery
2 tablespoons of raisins
3 tablespoons of low fat yogurt
2 teaspoons of mayonnaise
Cinnamon to taste

In a bowl, combine the first 4 ingredients and mix thoroughly. In a second bowl, combine the final 3 ingredients. Blend the 2 mixtures thoroughly and serve.

APPLESAUCE BROWNIES

1 cup of brown sugar
1 cup of white sugar
½ cup of applesauce
1 stick of butter, melted
2 eggs
1¼ cups of flour
¼ teaspoon of baking soda
¼ teaspoon of baking powder
1 teaspoon of cinnamon
1 teaspoon of vanilla
Cinnamon and sugar (to taste for topping)

In a large bowl, mix ingredients in the order listed. Pour batter into a greased 10-inch by 13-inch baking pan or dish. Sprinkle cinnamon and sugar on top to taste. Bake at 350 degrees for 30 to 40 minutes.

APPLES AND YAMS

4 yams, cooked and sliced
2 large apples, peeled, cored and sliced
1 cup of sugar
3 tablespoons of cornstarch
2 cups of water
1 stick of butter
2 teaspoons of lemon juice

In a pan combine cornstarch and sugar then stir in water, butter and lemon juice. Heat and stir until it thickens. Place yams and apples in a baking dish and pour sauce over them. Bales at 350 degrees for 40 minutes are until apples are tender.

BAKED APPLE

1 apple
1 tablespoon of orange juice
Cinnamon to taste

Core the apple but leave it whole. Place in a baking dish. Drizzle with orange juice and sprinkle with cinnamon. Bake at 375 degrees for 40 minutes.

BAKED BRIE & APPLES

3 apples, cut into wedges
8 ounces of Brie Cheese
¼ stick of butter, softened
¼ cup of almonds, slivered

Place Brie in a baking dish, Spread softened butter on top and sprinkle with almond slivers. Bake at 350 for 12 to 15 minutes. Serve on a platter with apple wedges.

BARBECUE SAUCE

½ cup of apple cider
½ cup of light brown sugar
¼ cup + 2 tablespoons of ketchup
1 tablespoon of flour
1 tablespoon of apple cider vinegar
½ teaspoon of paprika
½ teaspoon of salt
½ teaspoon of chili powder
¼ teaspoon of black pepper
¼ teaspoon of cayenne pepper
¼ teaspoon of onion powder
¼ teaspoon of garlic powder
Red pepper flakes to taste (optional)

In a pan whisk together apple cider and flour. Slowly stir in remaining ingredients and until thoroughly mixed. Cook over medium heat stirring while it cooks and thickens.

BEEF STEW

2 pounds of stew beef, cubes or chunks
1½ cups of beef broth
½ cup of flour
3 apples, peeled and diced large
4 carrots, chopped
1 yellow onion, diced
1 clove of garlic, diced
1 tablespoons of apple cider vinegar
1 teaspoon of Worcestershire sauce
1 teaspoon of curry

Put beef broth and flour in a slow cooker and mix thoroughly. Stir in remaining ingredients. Cover and cook on low for 10 to 12 hours or cook on high 4 to 6 hours.

CARAMEL APPLE CIDER

8 cups of apple cider
1 cup of caramel syrup
¼ cup of lemon juice
1 vanilla bean
6 inches of cinnamon stick, in pieces
1 tablespoon of whole allspice

In a slow cooker, combine apple cider, caramel syrup and lemon juice. Open a vanilla bean and scrape the seeds into the liquid. Place the vanilla bean, allspice and cinnamon sticks in a double thickness of cheesecloth. Tie up the spice bag and add to the slow cooker. Cover and cook on low for 3 hours. Remove the spice bag. Pour into mugs and top with whipped cream (optional).

CHOPS AND APPLES

4 pork chops, ¾ to 1-inch thick and trimmed
2 cups of water
1 cup of apple, peeled and diced
1 cup of celery, diced
¾ cup of rice
¼ cup of onion, diced fine
Salt and pepper
Oil

Salt and pepper chops to taste. In a skillet, brown chops in oil. Put the chops in a baking dish. Dissolve ½ teaspoon of salt in 2 cups of water. Pour water over the chops then spread rice evenly over the top. Cover with diced apple, celery and onion. Cover the dish and bake at 350 degrees for 50 to 60 minutes or until chops are tender.

CINNAMON APPLES

2 cups of sugar
1 cup of water
½ cup of cinnamon candies
4 drops of red food coloring
8 apples

Mix the first 4 ingredients together and bring to a boil. Peel apples and slice into quarters. Place apple pieces in the liquid and cover. Reduce the heat and simmer. Turn the apples occasionally and cook until tender and transparent.

FRUIT KABOB

3 peaches, quartered
3 bananas, sliced thick
2 apples, cut into wedges
1 pineapple, cut into large cubes
Wood skewers

SAUCE:
1 cup of grapefruit juice
2 tablespoons of Cointreau
½ cup of honey
½ teaspoon of fresh mint, diced

Mix the sauce ingredients thoroughly. Marinade the fruit pieces in the sauce for 30 to 45 minutes in the refrigerator. Alternate the fruit pieces on the skewers. Grill or broil the kabobs for 5 to 8 minutes. Baste with the sauce during cooking.

HOMEMADE APPLE SAUCE

10 apples, peeled, cored and sliced
½ cup of water
½ cup of sugar
½ cup of brown sugar
2 tablespoons of cinnamon
1 teaspoon of nutmeg
½ teaspoon of ground cloves
1 tablespoon of butter
2 tablespoons of lemon juice

Place ingredients in the cooker and stir thoroughly. Cover and cook on low for 8 to 10 hours. Chill the sauce upon completion or spoon the warm mixture on vanilla ice cream.

HOT APPLE CRANBERRY CIDER

2 quarts of apple juice
2 cans of frozen cranberry juice concentrate
3 cans of water
¼ cup of sugar
2 oranges, sliced
6 cinnamon sticks
1 teaspoon of whole cloves

Combine all the ingredients in a pot and mix thoroughly. Simmer over low heat for 1 hour.

MEATLOAF

1 pound of ground beef
½ pound of ground pork
1 cup of Cheddar cheese, shredded
½ cup of breadcrumbs
½ cup of quick cooking oats
½ of onion, diced fine
¼ cup of apple, diced fine
1 egg
2 tablespoons of Worcestershire sauce
½ teaspoon of salt
¼ teaspoon of pepper

In a bowl, thoroughly mix beef, pork apple, egg, onion, Worcestershire sauce, salt and pepper. Add Cheddar cheese, breadcrumbs and oats and remix again until ingredients are evenly distributed. Form the meat into a greased loaf pan. Bake at 350 degrees for 1 hour. Let meat rest 10 to 15 minutes before slicing.

PEAR & APPLE CIDER

2 cups of sweetened pear juice
1 cup of apple cider
1 cup of pear nectar
2 cinnamon sticks
3 allspice, whole

Combine pear nectar, pear juice, apple cider and cinnamon sticks in a pan. Put allspice in a piece of cheesecloth and tie it up. Put it in the pot. Heat mixture on low for 25 to 35 minutes. Strain the mixture. Serve warm or ice.

PORK CHOPS WITH APPLESAUCE

6 pork chops
2½ cups of applesauce
½ cup of sherry
¼ teaspoon of cinnamon
¼ teaspoon of nutmeg
Salt and pepper to taste
Oil

In a skillet brown the pork chops. Put the chops in a baking dish. Mix the applesauce, sherry and spices and spoon half of the mixture over the pork chops. Bake at 350 degrees for 20 minutes. Turn the chops and spoon remainder of the sauce on top. Bake for another 20 minutes.

SWEET APPLE QUICK BREAD

2 cups of flour
1 cup of apples, peeled and finely diced
1 cup of sugar
½ cup of butter, softened
½ cup of milk
½ cup of chopped nuts
2 eggs
2 tablespoons of orange peel, grated
1 tablespoon of corn syrup
1 teaspoon of baking soda
½ teaspoon of baking powder

Thoroughly blend all of the ingredients except the nuts. Beat for 3 minutes then stir in the nuts. Pour the batter into a greased loaf pan. Bake at 325 degrees for 50 to 60 minutes or until a toothpick tests clean.

For information on Tim Murphy's entire series of "Flannel John's Cookbooks" visit www.flanneljohn.com.

Printed in the USA
CPSIA information can be obtained
at www.ICGtesting.com
LVHW022149090923
757754LV00012B/659

9 781542 310680